THE CHEMISTRY OF SOAPS AND SALTS

CHEMISTRY BOOK FOR BEGINNERS

Children's Chemistry Books

BABY PROFESSOR

EDUCATION KIDS

In this book, we're going to cover the chemistry of soaps and salts. So, let's get right to it!

Table Salt

When you think of salt, you probably think of the table salt we use every day in our food. In chemistry, there are lots of different compounds that are salts. Salts come in many different tastes and colors, but not all of them are safe to eat. Salts are a combination of an acid and a base. They can also be made by combining an acid and a metal.

Sour

If you've ever had a sip or two of lemon juice before sugar was added to make lemonade, then you know how sour acid is. The word "acid" is derived from the Latin "acere," which simply means sour. The acids that we taste in liquids are natural acids.

An example of a base is the common baking ingredient sodium bicarbonate, more commonly called baking soda. If you mix it with a little water and rub it between your fingers, you would notice that it almost feels soapy. In fact, baking soda is not only used in baking, its texture and properties make it useful as a cleaner as well. You can use it with water to brush your teeth, as long as you don't swallow it. Of course, it's very bitter tasting.

Baking Soda

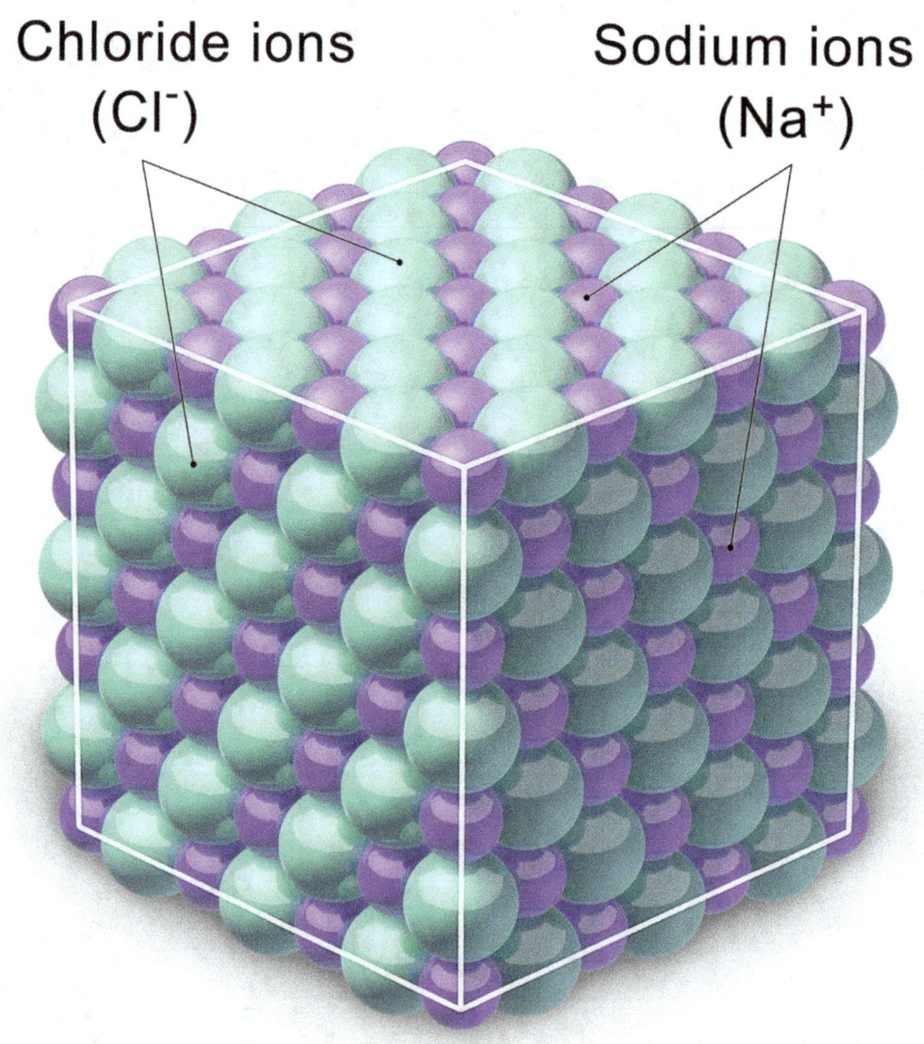

Dodium Chloride Crystal

When chemists talk about salts they are talking about ionic compounds. These compounds are created from a neutralization reaction when an acid and a base combine together. The reaction of these two substances causes water and salt to form.

Salts have certain characteristics. Most of these compounds dissolve in water. At room temperature, they are solids.

- ➡ They have strong chemical bonds.
- ➡ Their boiling points are relatively high.
- ➡ They are electrically neutral because they have an equal number of negative ions and positive ions.
- ➡ When they are the solid state of matter, they organize themselves in a lattice, which Is a rigid structure.

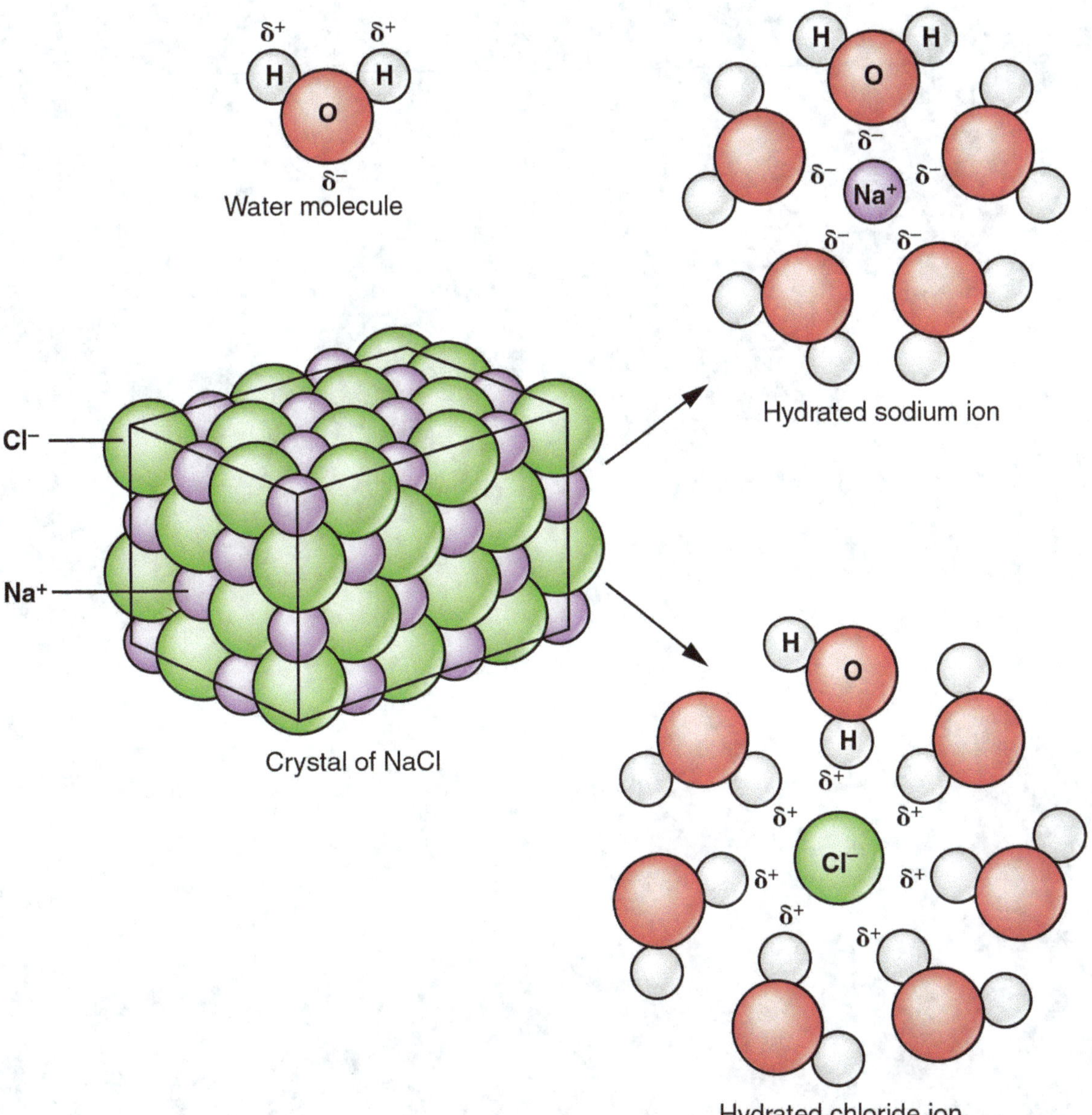

Ionic Compounds of Salt

Table Salt

SODIUM CHLORIDE OR TABLE SALT

The table salt that we use everyday is called sodium chloride. Its chemical formula is written as NaCl. The Na stands for the element of sodium and the Cl stands for the chloride. Table salt dissolves in water very easily. Sodium chloride is critical to life on Earth. In fact, the first life on our planet started out in ocean saltwater.

Table salt has been used for thousands of years as a way to preserve food as well as to give it added flavor. In Ancient times it was used as a form of money. The Romans gave a salary, called salarium, to citizens who did their work well and were "worth their salt."

Salarium

Salt Production

Salt production is a huge industry. There are three common methods for obtaining salt:

- Mining of salt underground by methods that are similar to coal mining
- Evaporation of seawater using the power of the sun
- Evaporation of the brines that come from pumping water into a deposit of rock salt

Additional purification of the salt is needed if it's going to be used either for flavoring or preservation of food.

The table salt we use is ground into very fine granules. If it's humid, salt tends to get caked together. Magnesium carbonate is added to table salt to prevent the salt granules from sticking together.

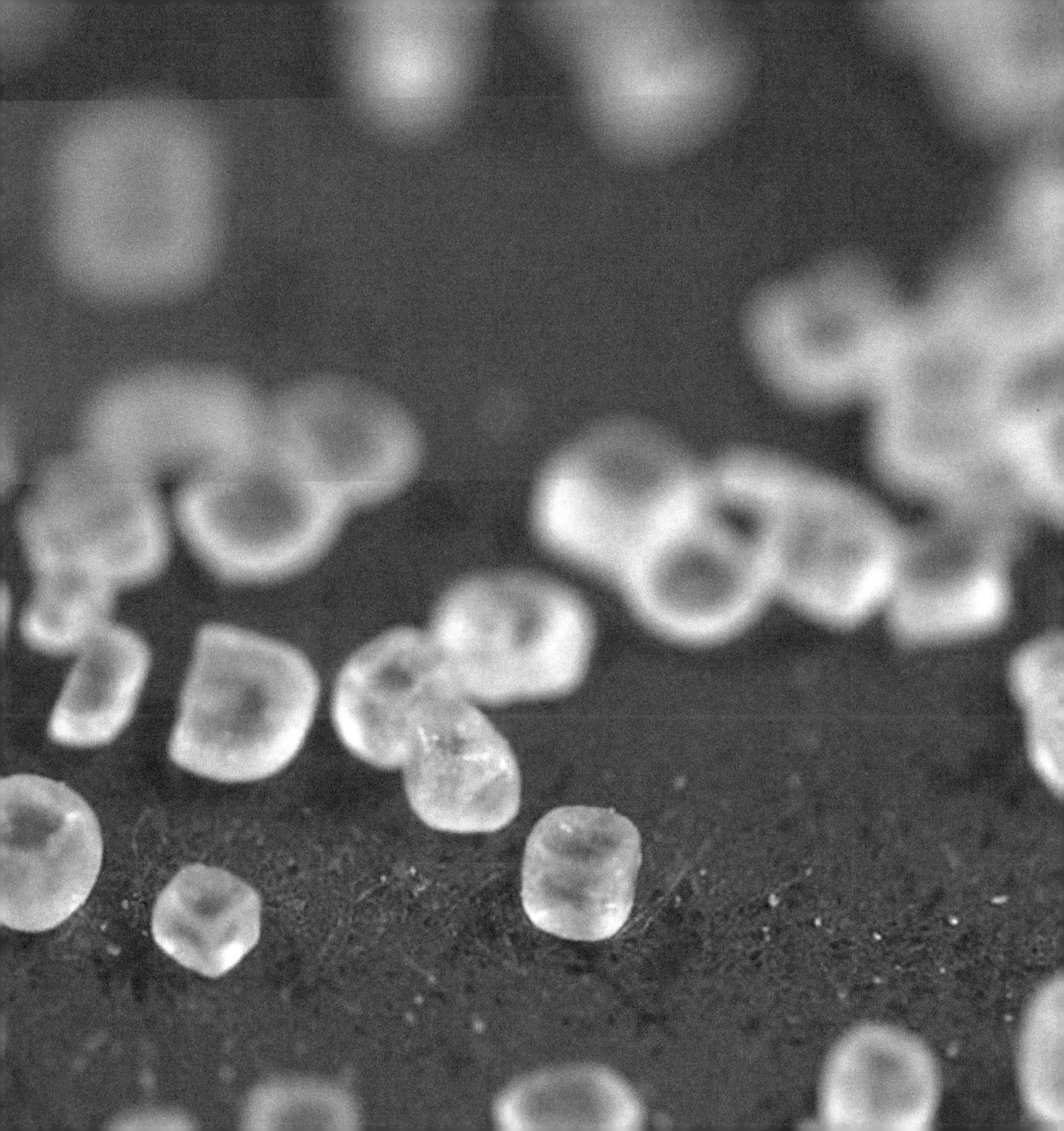

Most commercial salt is an iodized version since it was found that it was an easy way to get iodine, which is essential for proper thyroid function, into our diets. Since 1924, this addition has prevented many cases of goiter, an enlargement of the thyroid gland.

Over 200 million tons of table salt are produced each year with the countries of China and the United States being the biggest producers. We use a lot of salt on our food and in our food products!

Chinese Salt Farmers

Table Salt

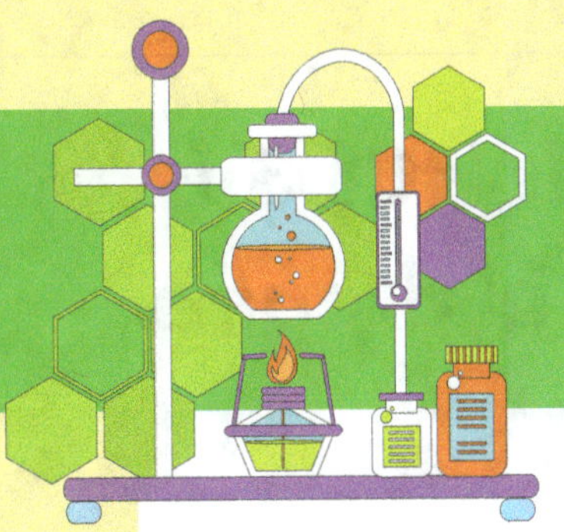

There are two different ways that salts can be classified. Salts can be classified as normal salts, acid salts, or basic salts.

Normal Salt - Table salt, also called sodium chloride, doesn't have hydrogen or hydroxyl in its chemical composition so it's called a normal salt.

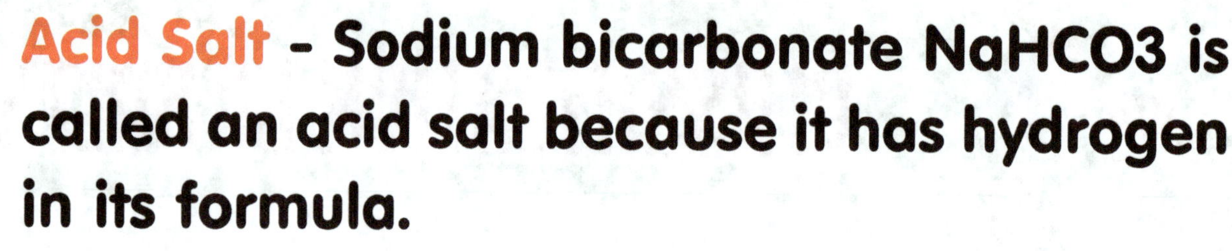

Acid Salt - Sodium bicarbonate NaHCO3 is called an acid salt because it has hydrogen in its formula.

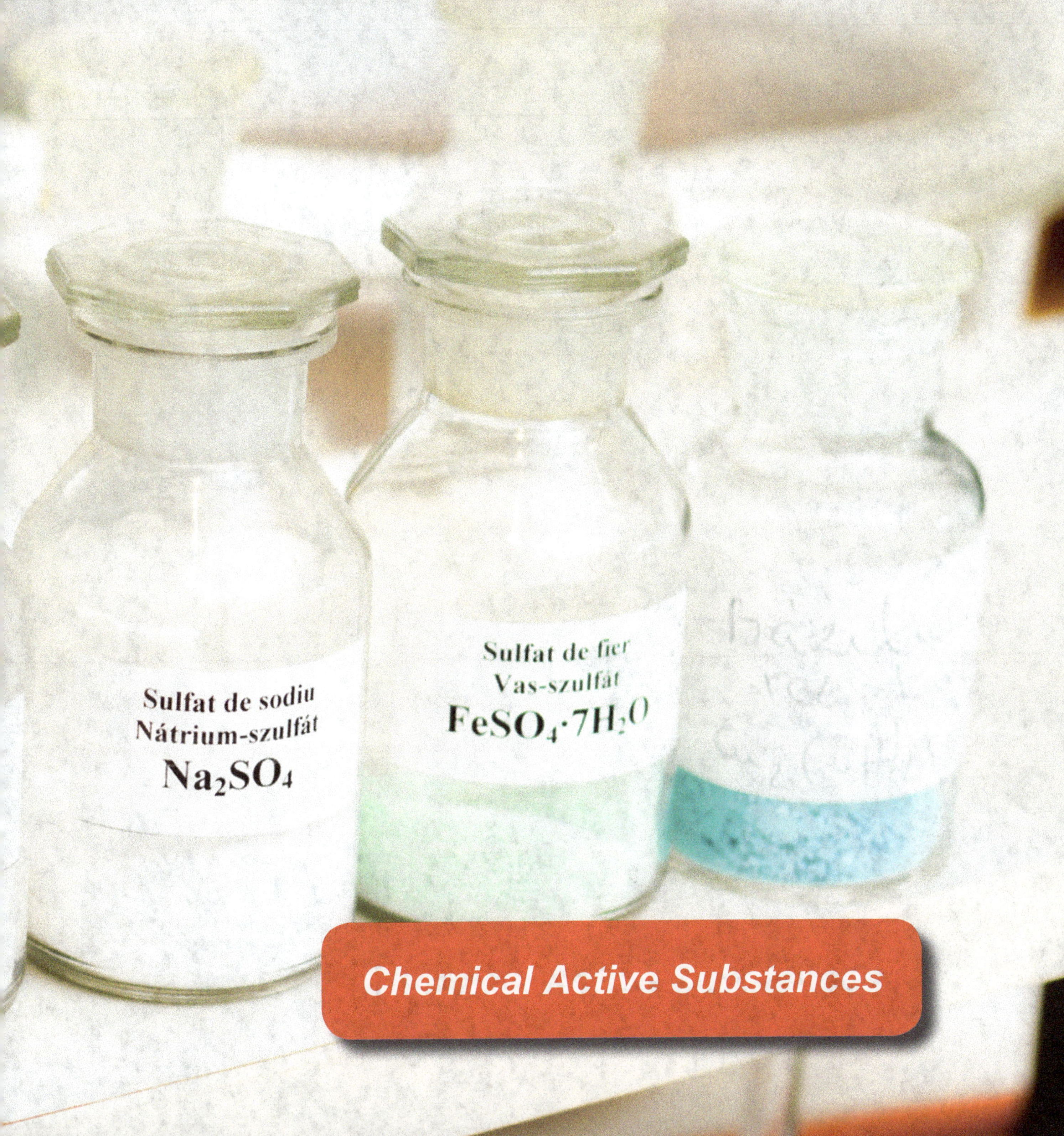

Sulfat de sodiu
Nátrium-szulfát
Na₂SO₄
Sulfat de fier
Vas-szulfát
FeSO₄·7H₂O
Chemical Active Substances

Basic Salt - Basic lead nitrate is called a basic salt because it had hydroxyl in its formula.

Salts can also be classified as simple, double, or complex. Simple salts, table salt is an example, have only have one kinds of positive ion, with the exception of the hydrogen ion in acid salts. Double salts have two different positive ions. Examples of double salts are calcium magnesium carbonate as well as the mineral dolomite.

Himalayas Salt

Alum Powder

nother special kind of double salt is an alum. For example, the compound aluminium sulfate is a double salt that is used in water purification as well as for dyeing and printing cloth. A complex salt, such as potassium ferricyanide is made up of a complex ion that doesn't come apart in a solution.

SOAP IS ACTUALLY A SALT

Soap is created by the reaction of an acid with a base. It's a salt of a compound that is a fatty acid. It's strange to think of soap as a type of salt, but that's what it is. Of course, it isn't an edible salt!

Soap

Bath Soap

We use soaps and detergents every day to clean ourselves, wash our dishes, and wash our clothes. The cleaning action of soaps and detergents come from their ability to take materials that can't be dissolved in water, such as oil or grease, and hold them suspended in water. It's the molecules in these cleaning agents that create this effect. The molecules form clusters called micelles.

For example, suppose you're trying to clean oil off a kitchen surface. When you add soap and water, part of the soap's molecules are attracted to the grease you're trying to clean and the other part is attracted to the water.

The grease is basically broken down by the alkyl groups of the soap molecules. At the same time, the ionic end makes it possible for the micelle to dissolve in water. The result is that the grease is emulsified in water and then can be rinsed away leaving you with a grease-free countertop.

THE HISTORY OF SOAP

People have always wanted to get clean. Before soap was invented, people would wash in rivers and streams. This got the dirt off, but didn't really get rid of grease. The earliest record of soap being made is from around 2800 BC. A soap-like material was found in pottery jars from the ruins of the Babylonian Empire. The inscription on the jars gives the recipe for the soap and says it was formed by boiling fats from animals with ashes. It was used for styling hair!

Aleppo Soap

Ancient Egyptians Bathing a Baby

The Egyptians used soap they created to bathe around 1500 BC. They made soap using oils from both vegetables and animals. They mixed these with sodium carbonate or other types of alkaline salt. The mixture was kind of goopy and worked well for cleaning as well as treating skin diseases. They bathed regularly and for an Ancient civilization their citizens were quite clean.

The Ancient Greeks used soap to wash their clothes but not their bodies. They scrubbed their skin with blocks of clay, pumice, and sometimes ashes to remove the grime. Then they massaged in different oils and used a special blade called a strigil to scrape it away.

Strigil

round 300 BC, the Ancient Romans made soap popular again when they built the first public baths in Rome. These baths were filled with water from their sophisticated aqueducts. They invented indoor plumbing but used toxic lead pipes. The citizens of Rome liked cleanliness.

When the Roman Empire came to a close around 460 AD, people stopped washing. Their homes became unsanitary. They were dirty and their food was contaminated. The lack of sanitary conditions brought out the plagues of the Middle Ages. Around 1300 AD, the plagues began. One third of Europe's population was killed by the bubonic plague that spread from China to Europe from traders traveling from Italy.

Plague Outbreak

Depiction of the Plague Outbreak

It took a long time for people to discover that their lack of cleanliness was causing diseases to run wild. In the 17th century, keeping conditions sanitary came back into vogue. Only the elite and the wealthy could afford soap. Soap makers guarded their secrets carefully so they could make the most profit. Soap and other detergents for cleaning didn't become easily affordable for the common citizen until the 19th century.

The early pioneers in America made their own lye soap for cleansing. It was inexpensive to make but it was harsh on the skin. The lye came from ashes and they used pig fat called tallow. The process to make it took days and the soap was so toxic that it caused burns on their eyes and skin.

Homemade Lye Soap

Today we're so fortunate to just buy a bar of soap at the grocery store or a container of iodized salt to use in our cooking.

Awesome! Now you know more about the chemistry of soaps and salts. You can find more Chemistry books from Baby Professor by searching the website of your favorite book retailer.

Visit

BABY PROFESSOR
EDUCATION KIDS

www.BabyProfessorBooks.com
to download Free Baby Professor eBooks and view
our catalog of new and exciting Children's Books